Table of C

MW01708747

Introduction

M&A can transform a business overnight.

On the other hand, many deals fail to deliver their intended result.

The M&A industry needs a lot of work. It lacks standardization, and most practitioners are still working in silos. There are instances where people who have day jobs get pulled into buying a company and don't know what to do with it. Often, a team of employees are asked to integrate a company they had no idea existed the month prior. These are just some of the common trends that are happening, and why more than half of M&A transactions fail.

There is a better way to do deals.

During my ten years doing M&A advisory work, I wanted to learn more about helpful best practices, including M&A management software. This led me to develop my own project management tool for M&A, DealRoom, because billion-dollar deals aren't going to be managed in Excel Sheets forever.

In the interest of improving this software and learning more about the industry, I started reaching out to deal professionals to discover their challenges and pain points. Then, a friend of mine suggested recording these conversations for other people to hear, and the M&A Science podcast was born.

With the help of friends and colleagues, I was able to speak with high-level M&A professionals to not only teach me, but also to share their best practices with everyone listening to the show.

Understanding that not everyone could review all of my podcast episodes, I decided to compile the most helpful highlights, and to provide the M&A community with best practices for each stage of the deal lifecycle.

This book was written in order to make the best information more accessible. I also wanted to give credit to all the practitioners who generously gave their time in the interest of moving the industry forward. This book would not have been possible without their help.

Knowing how to efficiently perform deals will deliver significant value to your organization.

Let's get started.

CHAPTER 1

Biggest Challenge in M&A

Traditionally, corporate mergers & acquisitions (M&A) practitioners have always focused on strategies, valuations, and finding the right deal for their companies.

However, I've noticed a rising trend on the emphasis of integration planning more than ever before. Why? Companies are starting to realize the value of integration.

A successful deal can revolutionize a business overnight, but over half of successful deals fail to meet their projected value.

Frequently, they are unable to capture intended synergies, resulting in spin-offs and divestitures down the line.

This is largely because the people who created the investment thesis, valuation model, and intended synergies are not part of the integration team. Ultimately, this is where value leaks in the acquisition.

People are starting to realize that it is all about Integration. It can make value or break value.

> "The biggest problem is the lack of continuity between the corporate development team and the integration team.
>
> **Galina Wolinetz, Managing Director at Virtas Partners M&A Integration | Separations**

CHAPTER 1

Why M&A Integration Usually Fails

"Any time there's an acquisition that doesn't meet a certain threshold of size, it seems like it doesn't get the necessary attention that would be required for any other large transactions.

After the transaction gets signed, it seems like the senior leadership loses interest in running that integration program.

The transaction gets thrown over the fence to some management team, or whoever is able to catch it, and that group is either ill prepared, has to do this on top of their day job, or lacking the tools, processes and resources that they should be using in order to achieve successful integration."

Galina Wolinetz, Managing Director at Virtas Partners M&A Integration | Separations

Also, every transaction is unique. Traditional M&A has always relied on playbooks, checklists, and templates. This approach is inefficient because every company will have different people, cultures, and challenges.

The dependence of the traditional approach on playbooks will cause oversight, which leads to bigger problems down the road.

CHAPTER 1

The Shortcomings of the Traditional Approach

"When you have more of a process and checklists, then people start to follow the checklist and work down the list, which is a fantastic feeling that you're getting things accomplished.

However, that basically means that you're not stepping back and thinking about the bigger picture.

Pilots have rigorous checklists, but there's also a stage when a pilot walks around the aircraft and does a general assessment outside of the checklist to make sure that they're ready to fly.

If everybody is thinking about the checklist, then no one is thinking about what is not on the checklist."

James Harris — Principal, Corporate Development Integration at Google

CHAPTER 2

Agile M&A

Forward-thinking M&A practitioners have been implementing an integration focused process called Agile M&A.

It's about being flexible and continually adjusting depending on the needs of the situation, not blindly following checklists. This is the new way of M&A.

The Agile methodology is specifically designed to eliminate many of the risks associated with contemporary M&A initiatives.

A new model for M&A comes with a new mindset. Instead of focusing on pre-planned cost synergies, Agile M&A is based on continuously discovering and capturing value.

It's all about harmoniously integrating the newly acquired capabilities with people in a way that preserves culture, and ultimately preserves value.

> "Agile is perfect for integration because integration never goes exactly the way you think."
>
> **Steve Elliott, Head of Jira Align at Atlassian**

CHAPTER 2

Agile Approach

"If you want to be a more future-oriented M&A professional, you need to take an Agile approach to things.

So think transformation, not transaction.

It's about leveraging the opportunities from a deal, but to do that you need to take a much more of a transformational mindset, as opposed to a transactional view.

Think opportunity and not just continuity. Think transformation value and not just transaction value. Live and breathe risk and not just trying to minimize it.

Above all remember this: the transactional approach to M&A will not deliver transformational results. The old ways are truly over!"

Toby Tester, Senior Consultant and Project Manager at BTD

CHAPTER 3

Deal Sourcing

Deals can come from anyone. They can come directly from your CEO, from the corporate development team itself, or even from a sales rep who knows someone at a company that is ready to sell. It doesn't matter where the deal comes from; what matters is that it aligns with your company's overall strategy. If you do not know why you are buying a company, capturing its true value will be extremely difficult.

Aligning Strategy With Your M&A Process

"M&A by itself is not a strategy. Many times, in the absence of a strategy, companies will try to buy their way into one. That's a common mistake that you see operating executives make. I really view M&A as a tool.

It's a really powerful tool that can help achieve and accelerate a company's strategic objectives."

Sean Corcoran, former Senior VP of Corporate Development and M&A at Neustar, Inc.

CHAPTER 3

Creating a List of Your Potential Targets

You have to keep the company strategy in mind when you are creating your own list. This will serve as your filter so your list will not become too long, but don't keep it too small. Keep your emotions out of it! Sometimes we are subconsciously biased towards specific companies that have personal connections to us.

Creating a List

"Build a good list of targets first. Don't start so broad that you're trying to boil the ocean; not every company in the world is a target.

Also, don't get so narrow that you only have a few names on your list; it's going to be a pretty short process to contact those companies.

Find the information to populate your database, whether it's from industry association lists or other lists that are available; whether they're free through internet searches, or sometimes you have to pay for the lists.

Improve the information in your database so each record makes sense from a corporate development standpoint.

That means finding out who the owners of each company are and any other useful info you can gather (such as size of the company, location and contact info). Your corporate development efforts will be off to a great start if you have a great database of targets."

Scott Kaeser, Head of Corporate Development at First Choice Dental Lab

CHAPTER 3

Leveraging Your Network

Maintaining relationships with a diverse set of people can help you source deals. Build trust and engage with people that can help you down the road. You can also educate them on what you do. This way, they will remember you when they reach that company's inflection point and want to do a deal.

A critical, but often neglected relationship is with the deal sponsor. You need to understand their mindset, perspective, and goals so that you know what kind of deals you should be exploring.

Relationships Needed by Corp Dev

"The relationship of the operating sponsor and the investment sponsor needs to be symbiotic. That is the secret sauce at J2.

We are very focused on giving the operators of our business independence and encouraging them to go out and acquire and use M&A capital.

The partnership between the M&A team and the operating sponsor is critically important.

We have a pretty structured approach in our M&A program where we have a pretty detailed funnel and stages of a deal; and at each stage, there's a different level of partnership between the corporate development sponsor and the operating sponsor."

Sean Alford, SVP, Corporate Development at J2 Global

CHAPTER 4

Targeting

As you are scouting your list for the next company you want to acquire, it is important to understand that not every deal is the right deal.

Sometimes, timing is a crucial factor when considering who to acquire. There are companies that may have been appealing six months ago, or may be appealing two years down the line.

Finding the Right Deal

“Just because there is an opportunity that surfaces to the top of your list, does not mean that you are going to close that deal.”

Dan Menge, Senior Director, and Head of M&A Integration at Xilinx

Early Diligence

You should also start doing due diligence at this early stage. You can use public information and start looking at the company’s core competencies, background, hiring processes, or even if they have legal issues, past or present. In this day and age, you can find pretty much anything about a company’s past on the internet, or even on social media.

CHAPTER 4

Doing Diligence During Targeting Phase

"You can look at the target company's website; I'm going to understand what they say about themselves and learn their core competencies.

I'm probably going to look at their press releases.

I'm going to look at their 'About Us' page. I also want to understand what their hiring and recruiting needs are because that'll give me a pretty good sense of how they're positioned in the market.

I'm going to look at social media; so I'm going to look at GlassDoor. I might look at Yelp. I might look at some other websites that provide ratings on how the company is doing both with their customers and their employees.

I might pay a visit to LexisNexis or some analysts reports like what D&B has, or if there's some other types of information that I can get my hands on about the target company, just to get a sense of what they're looking at.

Sometimes there's been a big lawsuit or something, even though I can't necessarily get filings, but if a company is in big enough trouble, I can see what's going on there."

Klint Kendrick, Chair of the HR M&A Roundtable and HR M&A Leader at a Fortune 500 company

CHAPTER 4

Early Integration

It is also in your best interest to bring in your integration lead during the targeting phase. They can bring integration insights and criteria, that can help you picture the overall strategy as you are selecting your next target company.

If you are an integration lead, you need to engage with the corporate development team proactively. Get involved as early as you can. This will help you optimize the integration planning process, and will increase the overall chance of deal success.

Integration During Targeting Phase

"Integration should start at the targeting stage; because they should understand and include some of the integration criteria and components into the targeting criteria and profiling of a particular client that you want to target or acquire.

As you bring those integration criteria into the mix, it allows for a better valuation further down the line. It allows you to prevent any risks, and not fall into some of the pitfalls.

You don't want to end up in a situation where you've closed the deal and as you're going through the integration, you're opening up the bonnet and you're finding a lot of things."

Javid Moosaji, M&A Sales Integration Strategy at Paypal

Integration Lead's Opinion on When To Get Involved in a Deal

"You have to be actively engaged and constantly checking in with corporate development because their timelines start off really slow until you get to a Letter of Intent.

Then once the LOI is signed, everyone drops what they're doing for the deal. With that, I tried to involve myself as early as possible to know what's coming down the pipeline."

Johanna Tseng, Corporate Development, M&A Integration at Coinbase

Relationships With Sellers

After selecting your target company, one of the most important things you can do is cultivate relationships with potential deal targets. This can help you in every aspect of the deal because it builds trust between the two companies. These strong relationships can also help the sellers, because they will give sellers an idea of who you are, how you treat employees, and what you will do with their company after you acquire it.

"Relationships with potential targets drive everything from better diligence, better integration, easier negotiations, to a higher likelihood of getting the deal done."

Michael Frankel, SVP and Managing Director at Deloitte

CHAPTER 4

One of the best relationships to be had is the CEO to CEO relationship. This allows you to assess what type of person you will be working with post-close.

In some instances, the CEO has no intentions of being a part of the new company. This is better to discuss early on.

A strong CEO to CEO relationship is also a good way to retain the business leaders of the target company.

When you're doing a bolt-on type of deal, employing the CEO is important because they are the ones who are going to take care of the company after the deal closes.

Relationships With the Seller

"In order to have a successful negotiation as a corporate development professional, there's a lot of relationships all day.

You have to keep in mind that it's not just about winning the negotiation at all costs for Microsoft.

Obviously, my job is to do the best deal for Microsoft, but remember that the company and the people in it are going to become a part of Microsoft. I'm negotiating with somebody who is eventually going to be on my team.

The relationship you build with that person and making sure that you're building a transaction and an outcome that is good, not only for Microsoft but everyone such that you're going to have a happy, productive, and successful team of people that come into Microsoft, adds a layer of complexity that I enjoy."

Devorah Bertucci, Director, Corporate Development at Microsoft

CHAPTER 5

Diligence

M&A is a Lot Like Buying a House

"Once you've selected a place and you put in your preliminary offer or your letter of intent, from there you move into the home inspection process which is due diligence.

Integration planning is just like planning to move into your new home. And you're probably going to do that at the same time as you're going through your home inspection.

I know when I've purchased my home, I think about, okay, this is where I'll stick the couch. I really don't like that paint color, I really want to do something different with that kitchen light.

I'm already planning to move in, even before I've got the keys to the house at close."

Klint Kendrick, Chair of the HR M&A Roundtable and
HR M&A Leader at a Fortune 500 company

CHAPTER 5

One of the best approaches we are seeing is involving the integration lead in the diligence process.

A lot of times, we see diligence and integration as a separate workstream. This is where value is lost and integration plans fail.

For example, when a group of people decide to buy a company, they dictate the value of the company, close the deal, and then pawn off the integration to another group of people who have no idea of what the company is about, why they bought it in the first place, and how to integrate it.

This is why integration needs to start as soon as diligence begins. You need to have a separate workstream of integration alongside the diligence team.

Integration Lead Starting Early

"Our role (integration team) starts during diligence.

We are working and forming ideas, understanding the product, the customer market, etc. We are continually iterating on the integration plan as we find more information."

Christina Amiry, Head of M&A,
Strategic Operations at Atlassian

CHAPTER 5

Planning Integration Early

"I'm a big fan of the integration being seen as another diligence track from the start, where the final deliverable for that track is the integration plan.

This captures things that don't necessarily end up in a legal document, such as how fast or how slow you're going to integrate, and how many touchpoints to integrate.

It's super important because it feeds off of all of the other workstreams, and then as a document that is also a manifesto from all the diligence streams.

If you don't agree with what we're planning here, you should raise your hand, and do so early on in the process.

The lead integrator should not only have a relationship with the diligence team, but also the deal owner and seller."

Carlos Cesta, VP, Corporate Development/M&A at Presidio

Planning integration alongside diligence also makes sense because every finding could have integration implications.

Whether it's from an HR, legal, accounting, or even a leadership perspective, all of these things can affect the overall integration process.

CHAPTER 5

Bringing Integration Early in Diligence

“One of the biggest lessons that I learned on a couple of my first deals was we did not have that integration function attached at the hip with me from the minute we signed that letter of intent through the entire diligence process.

That created challenges in having a more smooth integration process. Involving an integration lead from very early in the diligence process is important because there are many things we learn that can have integration implications.

That visibility, that early in the process and as we are building up the integration plan, makes us smarter across each of the functions.”

Jeremy Segal, Senior Vice President
of Corporate Development at Progress

CHAPTER 5

Valuation

In the interest of being Agile and adaptable, valuation models also need to be iterative.

Because of the limited amount of information in the initial stages of a deal, you should develop a high-level valuation model. The goal is to model out the target with your working hypothesis for business drivers.

As you get more information, typically post-LOI, you need to have a more detailed valuation model that has revenues modeled out at the product, product market, customer segment level, and a volume price-based model.

Contrary to popular belief, diligence and integration actually frame the success of valuation.

Valuation needs to be adjusted all the time as you discover additional things in the process. The diligence and integration planning are the inputs, and the valuation is the output.

You should also avoid valuing a company for more than five years. This can lead to an incorrect earnout.

No one knows what will happen in such a long period of time, and the company's success will depend on how it is run.

Make sure that you are not over-excited to close the deal, as deal-fever is one of the biggest reasons for overpaying during an acquisition.

CHAPTER 5

A Rigorous Valuation Methodology

"At the end of the day, the valuation that your financial model produces is an output, but the inputs, diligence and integration planning, in many ways, are much more important.

More often than not, bad deals happen because either the due diligence wasn't thorough or the integration plan wasn't detailed enough, or wasn't followed.

Having a rigorous evaluation methodology keeps you honest and ensures that you're looking at not only the quantum, but also the timing of synergies and the performance of the base business."

Erik Levy, Group Head Corp Dev,
and M&A at DMGT PLC

CHAPTER 5

Valuing a Company Long Term

"Using the DCF model and valuing a company for 10 years is a joke. No one knows what's going to happen in 10 years, and then you're putting a terminal value on it? It's just crazy.

You really can only know what's going to happen for a few years, and then it's going to be your choices; like what products are you going to do or what R&D is going to look like.

There's no way I know what business is going to look like after five years."

Brian Buchert, Vice President, Corporate Strategy and M&A at Church & Dwight

Aside from overpaying, some deals are just not a good fit. You need to learn when to walk away from a deal.

Some people are hesitant to walk away from an opportunity because they have already spent too much time on the deal; you have to remember that this is part of what you are trying to achieve in diligence - to find a reason not to do the deal.

CHAPTER 5

Walking Away from a Deal

"For folks who haven't been around M&A much, it can be a shock when you walk away from an opportunity that they put a lot of time and effort into.

However, it is part of the early education process for deal professionals to let their deal team know that this does happen on occasion. It should happen.

Frankly, it's part of what you're trying to achieve in diligence - to identify risks that would cause you to walk away from the deal.

If someone has been doing M&A for a long time and they have a hundred percent deal closure rate after signing a letter of intent, they're missing something.

There must be deals in their history that they shouldn't have done. Sometimes the best deals are the ones that don't get done."

Russ Hartz, VP, Corporate Development at Ansys

Culture

Culture is the way that things are done in an organization. It is arguably the most overlooked aspect of the diligence process.

Assessing culture early on can help you mitigate some of the risks, allowing integration to run smoother.

As you close a deal, it is very important to talk about the non-negotiables. There are certain aspects that you, as the acquirer, don't want to change in the acquired company because that is what will preserve the spirit of the deal.

Also, there are certain things that the acquired company cannot challenge because some aspects need to be preserved in your process, regulatory environment, product, etc.

Failure to cohesively combine two different company cultures is another reason why deal value may not live up to expectation, especially when a large company acquires a small one and these issues are unaddressed. Oftentimes, the small company ends up getting destroyed because of inefficient transitions.

The Importance of Culture

"Going back to Jack Welch's most significant podcast, he said it right there.

'The biggest mistake I've made when we acquired companies was when we made decisions purely based on numbers, and we didn't pay enough attention to culture.

In the end, the characteristics that make a company an attractive acquisition are reflected in the talent that you acquire and the way they get things done. You can conclude that in the end, the underlying reason for the deal is the talent and the culture you are acquiring.'"

Valeria Strappa, Director and Healthcare Integration Leader at JP Morgan Chase and Co.

CHAPTER 5

Expert Opinion on Large Companies Destroying Small Ones

"I think the most common issues as far as large companies unintentionally destroying small ones are the layering in of the bureaucracies, the decision making, and the approval processes, which can take much longer.

There are reasons why those processes are put in place for larger companies, but for a smaller one, they don't all necessarily make sense.

A common example is applying a Shared Service overhead allocation to an acquired business. You've got a large IT organization, which works for the acquirer, but certainly wouldn't be justified for such a small company.

The acquired entity might have had one, maybe two people, managing most of their IT along with some outsourcing.

Now, absent any other direction, the acquirer's accounting department follows their processes and applies a significant allocation that the smaller entity didn't have before the acquisition.

That's just one of many examples of inefficiencies that you can introduce inadvertently."

Jeff Desroches, VP, Strategy and Corporate Development at VAT Group

CHAPTER 5

Leadership

Leadership is also a critical aspect of any deal. Everything begins and ends with leadership. Leaders are the ones who are going to encourage and implement new mindsets, behaviors, and new ways of working on deals.

Leadership

"*The most important factor of all is leadership. If you don't have the leadership, you have nothing. A failure in M&A is a failure in leadership. Period.*

If you don't have leadership then nothing else follows.

To be successful in this day and age, leaders must embody and act out Agile and innovative ways of working. This is what our leaders must do."

Toby Tester, Senior Consultant and Project Manager at BTD

This is why a leadership assessment should be a part of your diligence process. Some even look at the leadership assessment as early as the targeting phase. Understanding the kind of leader that the target company has will give you an idea of what kind of culture they have in their organization.

If a leader is a bad fit into your organization, oftentimes it's because they no longer want to be a part of your organization. It is really valuable to have this conversation upfront, because you can proceed with that knowledge and make changes accordingly.

Leadership Retention

"A disengaged leader who is biding their time until a retention payment is due can quickly become toxic and create retention risks within the organization.

Having transparent conversations with individual senior leaders during due diligence, understanding their personal aspirations and how that aligns with your intentions for them and their roles, will pay dividends.

It will allow the acquiring business to plan for the leader's departure - often with a short-term incentive based on transferring key knowledge and information to others - and it allows the leader a graceful exit post close."

Sallie Cunningham, Director,
People M&A at Apple

Middle managers are also extremely important to the deal because they are the change agents. They are the ones that are executing at the employee level, and they are the voice of the masses going up to senior leadership to make necessary changes. They are the ones that provide the feedback and deliver the message from South to North.

Go-To-Market Planning

At this point in the deal, the corporate development lead should start creating the go-to-market plan with the target CEO. There are a lot of decisions that need to be made that will dictate further actions down the road.

For example, if you don't know what type of customers you are serving with your new combined product, then you won't be able to have the right discussions regarding the new systems, people, skills, and processes necessary.

CHAPTER 5

Early Go-To-Market Planning

"Go-to-market planning is the first thing that you should be doing.

If you think about why we acquire a company, it's because you want to achieve some kind of inorganic growth.

You're going to do that by combining customers, products, or skill set. Therefore you need to start with that. You should always start with go-to-market planning because that's part of your target operating model and your set up.

You start with the customer, you start with the products, and then the rest of your organization's capabilities should align to that.

What are the consequences of not doing that? There's a number of things: you can see customer service levels dropping. You can see customer attrition, they're defecting. You can see a bit of a blurred role and responsibilities within teams.

Imagine you have two sales teams coming together and then two related operation teams coming together, if you don't integrate the products, the offering, or at least come to an agreement of how you're doing that, or when you are going to do it, you get confusion around roles and responsibilities."

Javid Moosaji, M&A Sales Integration Strategy at Paypal

CHAPTER 6

Post-Close

As soon as the deal closes and both parties have agreed on the sale of the company, word gets around. Most employees panic and this causes problems for you as the acquirer.

They either freeze and stop being productive, or jump ship as they receive new or better offers from other companies.

Relationships with Regards to Deal Sourcing

> "We've got to keep people motivated, engaged and happy. Money alone isn't enough to keep people around. We gotta do a lot more than that.
>
> **Christina Ungaro, VP,**
> **Head of Corporate Development at Wind River**

CHAPTER 6

Day One

The first day after the acquisition, you need to make a good impression on your new employees. If you want them to trust you, you need to be as transparent as possible. This is their livelihood, and they want to know what will happen next.

Be clear in the early stages about why you're doing the deal, how you plan on onboarding employees, and what they should be expecting.

Be transparent about what will happen with the employee pay and benefits, because if you can't assure them what's going to happen, they will become disengaged. Show them that they matter, you care for them, and that they are more than just a number on the payroll.

You can also cultivate a relationship with an internal leader of the acquired company. Someone that can champion the upcoming changes and maintain a positive outlook of what's happening in their company.

The worst thing you can do is ignore the people who have a negative outlook on the entire deal. Their apprehensive feelings could start to influence others.

Try to talk to these people and address whatever questions they might have regarding change management.

> "Having key contacts within the acquired company and identifying those who have a more positive outlook can be key to urging the acquisition to have a more positive outlook. A lot of messages can sometimes have a bigger impact if they come internally or from someone they trust."

Briana Elkington, Sr. Manager, M&A Integration Management Office at Community Psychiatry

The Importance of Internal Communication

"You want to start building trust with those employees that have concerns.

If you have someone who's particularly outspoken in a negative way asking questions at a town hall or a training event, answer their questions.

If you don't know the answer to the question, let that person know that you don't know and that you'll find out and then find an answer and get it to them. You want to be the person who understands what's difficult about this transition and helps make it as less painful as it can possibly be."

Briana Elkington — Sr. Manager, M&A Integration Management Office at Community Psychiatry

Integration

Integration is often the most difficult part of the entire M&A process. This is the team that is tasked to deliver all the promises that the corporate development team made.

A well-managed integration can make the transition smoother, and can capture the acquired company's value to its fullest potential.

In order to make integration a lot smoother, an Agile approach is the best practice. And it's not just about processes, but being Agile as a mindset. It's important to be flexible and adaptive with the new working environment.

As I am sure you've heard before, integration is just like marriage. It is important to enter that integration phase with the proper mindset. It is not a competition.

You need to work with the acquired company. At the end of the day, these people will be part of your company, and they are the ones that are going to deliver value for you.

You have to find the balance between what your company wants to do, and what the acquired company is saying while achieving synergies and objectives.

Listen to the acquired company. They are experts in their field, which is why you bought them in the first place. Who knows, you might actually learn new best practices from the acquired company.

Agile Mindset

> "Whatever tools you have, if you don't have willing participants and people that are open to that type of working model, it's not going to work."
>
> **Christina Amiry, Head of M&A Strategic Operations, Integration at Atlassian**

CHAPTER 6

Cultural Integration

"I come from large institutions that have very well defined rates for execution and there's no need to discuss how things get done.

Then all of a sudden, we get challenged by the acquired company and we realize, wouldn't we be much better if we embraced that behavior or that process or that best practice.

Oftentimes, the acquirer is so concerned about integrating that it could be suffocating the assets that they acquired, losing the opportunity to advance together and even move your own company forward by learning from the new acquisition.

It's really important to keep eyes wide open to embrace change from both ends of the integration."

Valeria Strappa, Director and Healthcare Integration Leader at JP Morgan Chase and Co.

It is absolutely critical that everyone understands the rationale behind the deal.

This is the best way to keep your teams aligned, especially when integration can take years to finish.

To fully understand the strategy, you have to simplify things and let them know what you are trying to achieve.

CHAPTER 6

Creating an Environment for Success

According to Christina Amiry (Head of M&A Strategic Operations, Integration at Atlassian), in order to create an environment that fosters success for both sides, you need to consider four things.

1. **Have an Agile and adaptable approach**
    - Once you get that mindset, you will be more open to change. Realize that the acquired team can help you establish new processes.
2. **Immerse yourself in their culture**
    - Do your best to really try to learn from the people, understand the challenges of the business.
3. **Focus on tools**
    - Help them unlock their potential by teaching them how to use your products. This will accelerate your onboarding process, setting transparency and trust early on.
4. **Focus on people**
    - Have a leadership kickoff where you bring all of your functional leaders together with their counterparts in the acquired company, get to know each other better.

CHAPTER 6

A Story of an Integration Problem

“*We purchased a company in one of my prior employers that built drones.*

Their procurement process was they would go down to Napa auto parts and they would buy the pieces that they needed to build these prototype drones.

From there, you pull them into a large organization. That's a government contractor that has very specific rules about how you buy things.

All of a sudden a process that used to take two hours now takes weeks because you have to get supplier approval.

You have to make sure that the part is in the catalog. These are important elements of culture that often get overlooked. Then when you get into operating the post-integration business, all of a sudden, you're wondering why you're not delivering things on time.”

Klint Kendrick, Chair of the HR M&A Roundtable and HR M&A Leader at a Fortune 500 company

CHAPTER 6

Post-Integration

Even after the deal is finished, learning never stops. The best thing that you can do after a deal is a retrospective. Retrospectives are meetings with the purpose of reviewing what is working well and what is not, as well as considering how to improve on the process.

The goal of a retrospective is to gauge the effectiveness of the deal processes and tools to determine a plan for future improvement.

You can even do retrospectives in the middle of a particular phase of integration, or after you have completed specific deliverables or milestones.

Retrospectives can also be done in a set period of time such as monthly or bi-weekly. The higher frequency allows you to make more incremental improvements throughout the year.

Retrospectives

“In every deal that we do, we will do a retrospective. I am the first one to say, even though I have done this for over 20 years, that I am not perfect. I know that there are great lessons learned on every deal and things that we could do better. I think that is important.”

Jeremy Segal, Senior Vice President of Corporate Development at Progress

CHAPTER 6

M&A Center Of Excellence

If you want to take retrospectives even further and you want to capture/ maintain institutional knowledge, you could consider creating an M&A Center of Excellence.

An M&A Center of Excellence is a community of M&A professionals, who represent all functional areas, committed to developing and improving the overall M&A process of your organization. It's also a knowledge destination.

A repository of knowledge and tools for everyone to access for learning or contribution purposes.

Companies Developing a Center of Excellence

"There are four conditions under which building a center would be particularly valuable:

1. *When M&A is an important driver of your future growth strategy, and you have, or will have an active deal portfolio*
2. *When successful execution relies on leveraging knowledge across your enterprise*
3. *If you have enough commonality in strategy and approach across your business units to offer learnings that will benefit others*
4. *When you have the commitment and the bandwidth to take on the effort – building the center takes a lot of work and you need to be ready for it"*

Philip Pratt, Director of the M&A Center at Corning

CHAPTER 6

If your company relies on M&A as a growth strategy, then you should consider developing a center.

It can help you improve the ROI on your deals by achieving a cheaper, faster, and more effective integration process.

The repository can help you avoid repeating mistakes by leveraging past experiences, capturing that knowledge, and applying it to future execution.

ROI on Deal Efficiency

> "If you make a deal, the return on that investment really is dependent on how effectively you integrate it."
>
> **Philip Pratt, Director of the M&A Center at Corning**

CHAPTER 7

Conclusion

Once the deal closes, it's all about integration. Integration is where value is created or destroyed.

Failing to plan for integration early on can lead to missed value targets, teams working in silos, and the use of outdated practices and tools.

M&A doesn't need to be difficult. With the right structure, the right approach, the right level of enthusiasm, and if you are surrounded by the right people and tools, M&A can be fun and efficient.

Remember, M&A is a powerful tool that can exponentially grow your business. Don't waste opportunities and values.

If you are looking for best practices to improve your overall M&A process, be sure to visit our website mascience.com where we have compiled interviews with M&A professionals that share their experiences and proven techniques to increase deal success.

For a more detailed and evidence-based approach to M&A, you can check out our library of free plays **mascience.com/plays** that are designed to help teams revamp their deal lifecycle workflows. These plays are created by M&A professionals with a wide range of backgrounds and areas of expertise.

We have everything you need to make your M&A more successful, while continuously improving your deal lifecycle.

Here's to the deal!

M&A Science

Education and Technology for M&A

Visit **mascience.com** for free resources and to learn more about our business lines that make M&A better.

Product Portfolio

M&A Science Academy provides M&A training by leading practitioners. The academy includes on-demand training, certification, live training and networking events.

Agile M&A is the book that introduces an M&A management framework based on Agile principles. Agile M&A helps teams adopt techniques that drive efficiency and better outcomes.

M&A Plays is an open-source library of step-by-step techniques that are easy to learn and apply.

DealRoom is a lifecycle management software for M&A that enables teams to manage various transactions such as buy-side, sell-side, and fundraising, on one platform.

FirmRoom is the world's most intuitive virtual data room that complies with public company security standards.

About the Author

Kison Patel is the Founder and CEO of M&A Science, with a passion to drive the M&A industry forward.

He was an M&A advisor for ten years in which he sold larger companies such as commercial banks and hotel chains. In 2012, he noticed teams lacked efficient technology to manage deals and created DealRoom, an M&A lifecycle management platform.

In 2016, he started the M&A Science podcast devoting his time to creating a platform where all the best practitioners could share their best practices and lessons learned from real-life deals. Kison then created The M&A Science Academy in 2020 to offer step by step training to those looking to master M&A featuring courses created by top level practitioners. Through developing technology, educational content, and industry training, Kison aims to bring better practices to an industry with growing market pressures, transaction values, and competition.

kisonpatel.com

Appendix

1. Why is M&A Integration so Hard?
Galina Wolinetz, Managing Director at Virtas Partners
M&A Integration | Separations
mascience.com/library/why-is-m-a-integration-so-hard

2. How to Implement an Agile Approach into M&A
James Harris, Principal, Corporate Development Integration at Google
mascience.com/library/how-to-implement-an-agile-approach-into-m-a

3. Making Integration Successful from Both Sides of the Deal
Steve Elliott, Head of Jira Align at Atlassian
mascience.com/library/making-integration-successful

4. Aligning Strategy with Your M&A Process -
Sean Corcoran, former Senior VP of Corporate Development and M&A at Neustar, Inc.
mascience.com/library/aligning-strategy-with-your-m-a-process

5. Behind the Scenes: Effective Deal Sourcing and Closing
Scott Kaeser, Head of Corporate Development at First Choice Dental Lab
mascience.com/library/behind-the-scenes-effective-deal-sourcing-and-closing

6. Building a Partnership Between the Investment Sponsor and Operating Sponsor Sean Alford, SVP, Corporate Development at J2 Global
mascience.com/library/partnership-of-investment-and-operating-sponsor

7. The HR Practitioner's Guide to M&A Due Diligence
Klint Kendrick, Chair of the HR M&A Roundtable and HR M&A Leader at a Fortune 500 company
mascience.com/library/hr-guide-to-m-a-due-diligence

8. Leading M&A with Integration
Javid Moosaji, M&A Sales Integration Strategy at Paypal
mascience.com/library/leading-m-a-with-integration

Appendix

9. How Proactive Integration Engagement Can Differentiate Value in Deals
Johanna Tseng, Corporate Development, M&A Integration at Coinbase
mascience.com/library/proactive-integration-engagement

10. How to Cultivate Relationships with Deal Targets
Michael Frankel, SVP and Managing Director at Deloitte
Bruce Bowden, Chief Financial Officer at Bottomline Technologies
mascience.com/library/how-to-cultivate-relationships-with-deal-targets

11. Bridging the Gap Between Corporate Development and Integration
Devorah Bertucci, Director, Corporate Development at Microsoft
mascience.com/library/gap-between-corp-dev-and-integration

12. Making Integration Successful from Both Sides of the Deal
Christina Amiry, Head of M&A, Strategic Operations at Atlassian
mascience.com/library/making-integration-successful

13. Building a guide to project manage M&A
Carlos Cesta, VP, Corporate Development/M&A at Presidio
mascience.com/library/building-a-guide-to-project-manage-m-a

14. Building a Corporate Development Team with Contingencies
Jeremy Segal, Senior Vice President of Corporate Development at Progress
mascience.com/library/how-to-build-corp-dev-team

15. How Successful Diligence and Integration Planning Frames Successful M&A and Valuation
Erik Levy, Group Head Corp Dev, and M&A at DMGT PLC
mascience.com/library/successful-diligence-and-integration-planning

Appendix

16. Avoiding Valuation Surprises and Accounting for M&A Transactions
Brian Buchert, Vice President, Corporate Strategy and M&A at Church & Dwight
mascience.com/library/avoiding-valuation-surprises-and-accounting

17. 21 Dimensions to Cultural Integration
Valeria Strappa, Director and Healthcare Integration Leader at JP Morgan Chase and Co.
mascience.com/library/21-dimensions-to-cultural-integration

18. Why Big Companies Destroy Small Ones
Jeff Desroches, VP, Strategy and Corporate Development at VAT Group
mascience.com/library/why-big-companies-destroy-small-ones

19. Post Merger Innovation - don't just Integrate, Innovate!
Toby Tester, Senior Consultant and Project Manager at BTD
mascience.com/library/post-merger-innovation-dont-just-integrate-innovate

20. Tone at the Top - Intersection of Leadership and Culture in M&A
Sallie Cunningham, Director, People M&A at Apple
mascience.com/library/leadership-and-culture-in-m-a

21. Structuring Talent Focused Acquisitions
Christina Ungaro, VP, Head of Corporate Development at Wind River
mascience.com/library/structuring-talent-focused-acquisitions

22. Building an Effective Internal Communication Plan for M&A
Briana Elkington, Sr. Manager, M&A Integration Management Office at Community Psychiatry
mascience.com/library/building-an-effective-internal-communication-plan-for-m-a

23. How to Build an M&A Center of Excellence from Scratch
Philip Pratt, Director of the M&A Center at Corning
mascience.com/library/how-to-build-an-m-a-center-of-excellence-from-scratch

Learn from the best

If you enjoyed the M&A Tactics Handbook, check out M&A Science, a platform designed for M&A professionals to share knowledge and identify proven techniques. M&A Science comes in a variety of mediums, and many of the practitioners who contributed to this book are part of the M&A Science community.

M&A Science Podcast

What started in 2013 as research phone calls, transformed into an industry-leading podcast featuring practitioners sharing their lessons learned with over 20k listeners. Our listeners include corporate development professionals, private equity, investment bankers, consultants, and tech leaders. The M&A Science podcast is available on iTunes, Spotify, Google Podcasts, and Stitcher.

M&A Science Academy

The academy is an outcome-based online workshop program, providing clear and tangible value. Instructors demonstrate and encourage the practice of actual methods. Through this private community, you'll be able to move your practice forward by engaging with the greatest minds in the industry.

It includes how-to workshops, networking events, courses, educational ebooks, and templates. The workshops cover topics ranging from diligence, strategy, and integration. Learn how to build an integration playbook, plan and execute a divestiture, and how Agile M&A can transform your transaction process.

Visit **mascience.com** to learn more.

Here's to the deal!

Kison Patel
kison@dealroom.net